Old Enough To Know Better...

Young Enough Not To Care

Camilla & Rose

summersdale

OLD ENOUGH TO KNOW BETTER… YOUNG ENOUGH NOT TO CARE

Summersdale Publishers Ltd
46 West Street
Chichester
West Sussex
PO19 1RP
UK

www.summersdale.com

Printed and bound in the Czech Republic

ISBN: 978-1-84953-554-0

Substantial discounts on bulk quantities of Summersdale books are available to corporations, professional associations and other organisations. For details contact Nicky Douglas by telephone: +44 (0) 1243 756902, fax: +44 (0) 1243 786300 or email: nicky@summersdale.com.

To............Carol..

From............Marjorie...

My experience is that as
soon as people are old enough
to know better, they don't
know anything at all.

OSCAR WILDE

I don't need you to remind me
of my age, I have a bladder
to do that for me.

STEPHEN FRY

If you are finding ageing hard to swallow... just add more gin!

At middle age the soul should
be opening up like a rose,
not closing up like a cabbage.

JOHN ANDREW HOLMES

Don't let ageing get you down.
It's too hard to get back up.

JOHN WAGNER

Young at heart, slightly older in other places!

Inside every older person is a younger person wondering what the hell happened.

CORA HARVEY ARMSTRONG

The girls soon realised their topless sunbathing days were over!

If you obey all the rules,
you miss all the fun.

KATHARINE HEPBURN

Life has got to be lived.
That's all there is to it.

ELEANOR ROOSEVELT

Midlife, glass half empty feeling?
Time for a top-up!

I have reached an age when,
if someone tells me to wear
socks, I don't have to.

ALBERT EINSTEIN

The best part of the art of living is
to know how to grow old gracefully.

ERIC HOFFER

Old enough to know better, drunk enough not to care!

Age wrinkles the body.
Quitting wrinkles the soul.

DOUGLAS MACARTHUR

Oft from shrivelled skin comes
useful counsel.

SAEMUND SIGFUSSON

Getting old: when your skin eats more cream than you do!

Life is a moderately good play
with a badly written third act.

TRUMAN CAPOTE

The secret of staying young is
to live honestly, eat slowly
and lie about your age.

LUCILLE BALL

If things improve with age, you are approaching MAGNIFICENT!

One of the many
pleasures of old age
is giving things up.

MALCOLM MUGGERIDGE

After a man passes
60, his mischief is
mainly in his head.

EDGAR WATSON HOWE

He decided he was like a
fine wine and would age
much better on his side!

The older one grows,
the more one likes indecency.

VIRGINIA WOOLF

The young man knows the rules but
the old man knows the exceptions.

OLIVER WENDELL HOLMES JR

He wondered when his wild oats had turned to shredded wheat.

Just remember, once you're over
the hill, you begin to pick up speed.

CHARLES M. SCHULZ

You may hate gravity, but
gravity doesn't care.

CLAYTON CHRISTENSEN

Do you think I'll get a discount if I don't need the top?

I have the body of
an 18-year-old.
I keep it in the fridge.

she found her own way of
coping with the hot flushes!

Let us respect grey hairs,
especially our own.

J. P. SEARS

There is only one cure for grey hair.
It was invented by a Frenchman.
It is called the guillotine.

P. G. WODEHOUSE

Every time I find a new grey hair a fairy has to die!

The best way to get a husband to do anything is to suggest that he is too old to do it.

FELICITY PARKER

To stop ageing – keep on raging.

MICHAEL FORBES

This is not a beer belly, it's a
fuel tank for a sex machine!

No wise man ever wished
to be younger.

JONATHAN SWIFT

I'm aiming by the time I'm 50 to
stop being an adolescent.

WENDY COPE

Glad to see you still have
a spring in your step!

One of the many things nobody tells you about middle age is that it's a nice change from being young.

WILLIAM FEATHER

Time may be a great healer, but it's a lousy beautician.

ANONYMOUS

she knew she was getting older
when she tried to straighten
the wrinkles in her tights and
discovered she wasn't wearing any!

You know you're getting old
when your idea of hot, flaming
desire is a barbecued steak.

VICTORIA FABIANO

It's sex, not youth,
that's wasted on the young.

JANET HARRIS

They say love is blind, shame it still has a sense of hearing!

One should never make one's debut in a scandal. One should reserve that to give interest to one's old age.

OSCAR WILDE

Old age is an excellent time for outrage. My goal is to say or do at least one outrageous thing every week.

MAGGIE KUHN

Celebrate! You've got everything you had 20 years ago it's just a little bit lower now, that's all!

If you resolve to give up
smoking, drinking and loving,
you don't actually live longer.
It just seems longer.

CLEMENT FREUD

When it comes to staying young, a
mindlift beats a facelift any day.

MARTY BUCELLA

The bonus of getting older is alcohol can be regarded as medicinal!

They say that age is all
in your mind. The trick is
keeping it from creeping
down into your body.

ANONYMOUS

She was convinced she had cabinet fever as her chest had dropped into her drawers!

Men chase golf balls when they're
too old to chase anything else.

GROUCHO MARX

Boys will be boys and so will a lot
of middle-aged men.

KIN HUBBARD

When I asked if you wanted to
play around... I didn't mean...

I think your whole life shows
in your face, and you should
be proud of that.

The easiest way to diminish
the appearance of wrinkles
is to keep your glasses off
when you look in the mirror.

CHILDHOOD
The time of life when you make funny faces in the mirror.

MIDDLE AGE
The time when the mirror gets even!

I'm officially middle-aged. I don't need drugs... I can get the same effect just by standing up real fast.

JONATHAN KATZ

You know you are getting older when 'happy hour' is a nap.

GARY KRISTOFFERSON

Remember when shake, rattle and roll meant more than just getting out of bed?

One of the best parts of growing older? You can flirt all you like since you've become harmless.

LIZ SMITH

I can still remember when the air was clean and the sex was dirty.

GEORGE BURNS

Mmmm, darling, you shouldn't have... diesel and super unleaded!

To win back my youth...
there is nothing I wouldn't
do – except take
exercise, get up early,
or be a useful member
of the community.

OSCAR WILDE

My whole exercise routine
lasts an hour and a half...
15 minutes cardio, 15 minutes
weights, and an hour to
talk myself into it!

Growing old is compulsory,
growing up is optional.

BOB MONKHOUSE

Getting old is a bit like getting
drunk; everyone else looks brilliant.

BILLY CONNOLLY

They say wine improves with age;
the older I get the more I like it!

I'm too old to do things by half.

LOU REED

Every morning, like
clockwork, at 7 a.m., I pee.
Unfortunately, I don't wake up till 8.

HARRY BECKWORTH

Pulled again!

Each year it grows harder to make ends meet – the ends I refer to are hands and feet.

RICHARD ARMOUR

Middle age is when your age starts to show around your middle.

BOB HOPE

I bought some skinny jeans
but they don't work!

We do not stop playing because
we grow old. We grow old
because we stop playing.

Few women admit their age.
Few men act theirs.

The inbetweeners: too old to be irresponsible, too young to be eccentric!

You don't get older,
you get better.

SHIRLEY BASSEY

When grace is joined with wrinkles,
it is adorable. There is an
unspeakable dawn in happy old age.

VICTOR HUGO

She believed she was entering the metallic years: silver in her hair, gold in her teeth and lead in her bottom!

All would live long, but
none would be old.

BENJAMIN FRANKLIN

Time and trouble will tame an
advanced young woman, but
an advanced old woman is
uncontrollable by any
earthly force.

DOROTHY L. SAYERS

Old soak!

After thirty, a body
has a mind of its own.

BETTE MIDLER

It's important to exercise your pelvic floor regularly!

Laughter doesn't require teeth.

BILL NEWTON

Wrinkles should merely indicate
where smiles have been.

MARK TWAIN

The good news about midlife is
the glass is still half full...

The bad news is it won't be long
before your teeth are floating in it!

Middle age is when your broad
mind and narrow waist begin
to change places.

E. JOSEPH COSSMAN

It takes a long time to grow young.

PABLO PICASSO

When ageing takes its toll...

We are young only once, after that
we need some other excuse.

The key to successful
ageing is to pay as little
attention to it as possible.

...gravity is there right beside it!

Age seldom arrives
smoothly or quickly.
It's more often a
succession of jerks.

JEAN RHYS

When body parts start to creak,
reach for the lubricant!

There are three periods
in life: youth, middle age
and 'how well you look'.

I want to have a good body, but
not as much as I want dessert.

Of course I'm in shape - isn't round a shape?

I'm at an age where
my back goes
out more than I do.

PHYLLIS DILLER

Gravity can sometimes get in the way of a good time!

Not a shred of evidence
exists in favour of the idea
that life is serious.

BRENDAN GILL

The impotant thing... is not how
many years in your life, but
how much life in your years!

EDWARD STIEGLITZ

You may not be able to
turn back the clock, but
you can wind it up again!

If you're interested in finding
out more about our books,
find us on Facebook at
Summersdale Publishers
and follow us on Twitter at
@Summersdale.

www.summersdale.com